The Most Refreshing No-Bake Summer Desserts Cookbook

Decadent Sweet Treats to Let You Chill on Warm Days

BY: SOPHIA FREEMAN

Table of Contents

Introduction

Summer is always a great excuse to relax and eat refreshing foods to cool down. Although many of us rejoice in the endless possibilities summer may bring, it is somehow a different story when it comes to certain food cravings during the hot summer months.

We all know how a single baking session can easily heat up the entire kitchen, and that is the last thing you would want during an already humid day. But would you believe that you can make a cake even without an oven?

No-bake recipes do not require the use of an oven. They do, however, employ other methods like refrigeration, freezing and microwaving. These are food preparations born out of necessity and convenience as it typically requires only a handful of ingredients and is practically fuss-free.

Apart from this, no-bake recipes are suited for people who do not have an oven available. Plus, it's a super fun activity that is safe for the kids to enjoy.

Additional Useful & Interesting Information

Use good quality and fresh ingredients. For best results, make sure that the ingredients are at room temperature to get a better texture.

For recipes that need refrigeration, follow the required time indicated in the recipe to make sure that ingredients will set and keep its form.

The use of fresh and seasonal produce in the recipes will leave you feeling refreshed and give you a boost of essential vitamins and minerals. For example, berries are rich in antioxidants and low in calories. They contain properties that can help fight inflammation and improve blood sugar levels. Bananas are great for improving heart and gut health, while avocados are rich in vitamins K, C, A, B and E, and are wonderful sources of healthy dietary fiber.

Berry & Pistachio Pie

You don't have to wait for a special occasion to whip up this heavenly pie. At any time that you have berries, you don't know what to do with, this is always a great idea everyone in the family will love.

Serving Size: 10

Preparation & Cooking Time: 6 hours and 30 minutes

Ingredients:

- 3 oz. lemon gelatin
- 1 cup boiling water
- ¾ cup cold water
- 2 tablespoons lemon juice, divided
- 1 teaspoon lemon zest
- 4 cups whipped topping, divided
- ¾ cup pistachios, chopped
- 1 graham cracker crust
- 1 cup blueberries
- 1 ½ cups strawberries, sliced

For garnish

- Coconut flakes, toasted
- Pistachios, chopped

Instructions:

Add the gelatin to a bowl.

Pour in the boiling water.

Stir for 2 minutes or until the gelatin has dissolved.

Pour in the cold water, 1 tablespoon lemon juice, and lemon zest.

Cover and refrigerate for 2 hours.

Add 2 cups whipped topping to the gelatin.

Stir until smooth.

Stir in the pistachios.

Add the graham crust to a pie pan.

Add the gelatin mixture on top of the crust.

Cover and refrigerate for 4 hours.

Spread the remaining whipping topping on top.

Toss the blueberries and strawberries in the remaining lemon juice.

Add these on top of the pie.

Sprinkle with the pistachios and coconut flakes.

Nutrients per Serving:

- Calories 345
- Fat 18 g
- Saturated fat 9 g
- Carbohydrates 41 g
- Fiber 3 g
- Protein 4 g
- Cholesterol 0 mg
- Sugars 33 g
- Sodium 217 mg
- Potassium 252 mg

Strawberry Cooler

This easy-to-prepare no-bake dessert cools you off on a summer day, and at the same time, satisfies the cravings of your sweet tooth.

Serving Size: 3

Preparation & Cooking Time: 15 minutes

Ingredients:

- ½ cup water
- ¾ cup sugar
- 3 cups strawberries, hulled
- ¼ cup orange juice
- ¼ cup lime juice

Instructions:

Pour the water into a saucepan over medium heat.

Stir in the sugar.

Bring to a boil.

Stir until the sugar has been dissolved.

Transfer the syrup to a bowl and let cool.

Cover and refrigerate for 30 minutes.

Add the strawberries, orange juice, lime juice and sugar syrup.

Process to blend.

Pour the mixture into an ice cream maker.

Follow the manufacturer's instructions for processing the ice cream.

Serve or store in containers.

Nutrients per Serving:

- Calories 128
- Fat 0 g
- Saturated fat 0 g
- Carbohydrates 33 g
- Fiber 1 g
- Protein 1 g
- Cholesterol 0 mg
- Sugars 30 g
- Sodium 1 mg
- Potassium 162 mg

Key Lime Pie

This light and creamy pie won't leave you wanting. It satisfies your cravings for sweets without making you feel guilty afterward!

Serving Size: 8

Preparation & Cooking Time: 30 minutes

Ingredients:

- ¼ cup boiling water
- 1 packet lime gelatin
- 12 oz. key lime yogurt
- 8 oz. nonfat whipped topping
- 1 graham cracker crust

Instructions:

Pour the water into a bowl.

Add the lime gelatin.

Stir for 2 minutes or until dissolved completely.

Stir in the yogurt and then the whipped topping.

Place the crust in a pie pan.

Top the crust with the yogurt mixture.

Cover and refrigerate for 2 hours.

Nutrients per Serving:

- Calories 194
- Fat 3 g
- Saturated fat 1 g
- Carbohydrates 33 g
- Fiber 0 g
- Protein 3 g
- Cholesterol 2 mg
- Sugars 18 g
- Sodium 159 mg
- Potassium 46 mg

Italian Pineapple Trifle

This rich and creamy Italian pineapple trifle tempts you in more ways than one. For sure, the whole family will enjoy this dessert, and you'll love that it's easy to prepare.

Serving Size: 8

Preparation & Cooking Time: 4 hours and 30 minutes

Ingredients:

- 11 oz. cream cheese, softened
- 15 oz. ricotta cheese
- ¾ cup sugar
- 2 teaspoons vanilla extract, divided
- 2 cups heavy whipping cream
- 15 ¾ oz. lemon pie filling
- 16 oz. crushed pineapple
- 9 oz. ladyfinger cookies

Instructions:

Add the cream cheese, ricotta cheese and sugar in a bowl.

Stir in 1 teaspoon vanilla extract.

Beat until fluffy.

In another bowl, beat the heavy cream with an electric mixer until you see stiff peaks forming.

Stir in the cream cheese mixture.

In a third bowl, combine the pie filling and crushed pineapple.

Stir in the remaining vanilla extract.

In a trifle bowl, arrange the ladyfingers in the bottom and sides.

In the middle, make several layers of the cream cheese mixture, pineapple mixture, and the remaining ladyfingers.

Cover and refrigerate for 4 hours before serving.

Nutrients per Serving:

- Calories 455
- Fat 25.5 g
- Saturated Fat 15.4 g
- Carbohydrate 47.5 g
- Fiber 0.9 g
- Protein 10.6 g
- Cholesterol 140 mg
- Sugars 24.9 g
- Sodium 241 mg
- Potassium 188mg

Cannoli Dip

Cannoli dip is typically made with mascarpone cheese, ricotta cheese, vanilla extract, and confectioners' sugar. In this recipe, we place this mixture inside sugar cones for a dessert that's delicious and easy.

Serving Size: 8

Preparation & Cooking Time: 10 minutes

Ingredients:

- 7 oz. mascarpone cheese
- 8 oz. ricotta cheese
- ¾ cup confectioners' sugar
- 1 teaspoon vanilla extract
- 1 tablespoon lime zest
- 1 tablespoon candied citron, chopped
- Sugar cones
- Miniature chocolate chips

Instructions:

Combine the mascarpone cheese, ricotta cheese, confectioners' sugar, vanilla extract, lime zest and citron in a bowl.

Scoop the mixture into the sugar cones.

Sprinkle with the chocolate chips before serving.

Nutrients per Serving:

- Calories 128

- Fat 5 g

- Saturated fat 3 g

- Carbohydrates 16 g

- Fiber 0 g

- Protein 6 g

- Cholesterol 21 mg

- Sugars 15 g

- Sodium 70 mg

- Potassium 64 mg

Strawberry Pie

Here's a light but heavenly strawberry pie that you and your family can enjoy for a snack or after dinner. It's as good as you expect it.

Serving Size: 8

Preparation & Cooking Time: 3 hours and 30 minutes

Ingredients:

- 8 oz. canned crushed pineapple
- Water
- 3 oz. sugar-free strawberry gelatin
- 8 oz. sugar-free vanilla pudding mix
- 3 cups strawberries, sliced
- 1 graham cracker crust
- ½ cup low-fat whipped topping

Instructions:

Drain the crushed pineapple but reserve the juice.

Add the juice to a measuring cup.

Pour in water so that the mixture measures 1 and ½ cups.

Pour the mixture into a pan over medium heat.

Stir in the gelatin and pudding mix.

Bring to a boil.

Cook while stirring for 2 minutes.

Add the pineapple chunks.

Turn off heat and let cool.

Fold in the strawberries.

Add the crust in a pie pan.

Pour the mixture into the crust.

Cover and refrigerate for 3 hours.

Top with the whipped topping and serve.

Nutrients per Serving:

- Calories 159
- Fat 4 g
- Saturated fat 2 g
- Carbohydrates 29 g
- Fiber 2 g
- Protein 2 g
- Cholesterol 0 mg
- Sugars 14 g
- Sodium 172 mg
- Potassium 138.5 mg

Cherry & Amaretti Cooler

Amaretti refers to Italian almond macaroons that are either soft and chewy or thin and crispy. We make this heavenly dessert with crushed amaretti, dark sweet cherries, sour cream, and whipping cream.

Serving Size: 8

Preparation & Cooking Time: 2 hours and 30 minutes

Ingredients:

- 1 packet plain gelatin
- 1/3 cup cold water
- 2 cups dark sweet cherries, chopped and divided
- 1 cup sour cream
- 1 tablespoon lemon juice
- ½ cup sugar
- ½ teaspoon vanilla extract
- ½ teaspoon almond extract
- 1 cup heavy whipping cream
- 16 amaretti cookies, crushed

Toppings

- Cherries
- Fresh mint leaves

Instructions:

Add the gelatin in a saucepan.

Pour in the cold water.

Stir until dissolved.

Let sit for 1 minute.

Place the pan over low heat.

Heat through while stirring for 5 minutes.

Let sit for another 5 minutes.

Add 1 cup cherries, gelatin mixture, sour cream, lemon juice, sugar, vanilla extract and almond extract to a blender.

Process until pureed.

Transfer to a bowl.

Beat the whipping cream with an electric mixer until you see soft peaks forming.

Reserve ½ cup for topping.

Add the remaining whipped cream into the sour cream mixture.

Fold in the amaretti cookies and remaining cherries.

Pour the mixture into dessert dishes.

Refrigerate for 2 hours.

Top with the reserved whipped cream, fresh mint leaves and cherries.

Nutrients per Serving:

- Calories 323
- Fat 19 g
- Saturated fat 10 g
- Carbohydrates 36 g
- Fiber 1 g
- Protein 4 g
- Cholesterol 41 mg
- Sugars 32 g
- Sodium 112 mg
- Potassium 217 mg

Strawberry & Pretzel Pie

This is the dessert that makes you look like a pro. Your friends are going to think you spent a lot of time preparing this but in fact, this no-bake pie only takes 30 minutes of active prep time.

Serving Size: 16

Preparation & Cooking Time: 6 hours and 45 minutes

Ingredients:

- 4 cups miniature pretzels
- ¼ cup sugar
- 6 tablespoons butter, melted
- 6 oz. strawberry gelatin
- ¾ cup boiling water
- ¼ cup lemon juice
- 2 cups heavy whipping cream, divided
- 2/3 cup condensed milk (sweetened)
- 2/3 cup cream cheese, whipped
- 7 oz. marshmallow cream
- ½ lb. strawberries, chopped

For garnish

- Miniature pretzels
- Strawberry, sliced

Instructions:

Add the pretzels to a food processor.

Process until finely chopped.

Add the sugar and butter.

Process until fully combined.

Reserve 1/3 cup for topping.

Press the remaining pretzel mixture into a pie pan.

Cover and refrigerate for 30 minutes.

Add the gelatin to a bowl.

Pour in the boiling water.

Stir for 2 minutes to dissolve completely.

Add the lemon juice and stir.

Cover and refrigerate for 30 minutes, stirring every 10 minutes.

Beat half of the heavy cream with an electric mixer until you see stiff peaks forming.

Stir in the condensed milk, cream cheese and marshmallow cream.

Fold in the strawberries.

Add this mixture to the gelatin mixture.

Place the graham crust into a pie pan.

Pour the mixture on top of the crust.

Cover and refrigerate for 6 hours.

Beat the remaining heavy cream.

Spread this over the pie and top with the crushed miniature pretzels, whole miniature pretzels and sliced strawberries.

Nutrients per Serving:

- Calories 350
- Fat 19 g
- Saturated fat 12 g
- Carbohydrates 39 g
- Fiber 1 g
- Protein 4 g
- Cholesterol 56 mg
- Sugars 30 g
- Sodium 284 mg
- Potassium 187 mg

Berry Tiramisu

One taste of this delectable dessert and it instantly becomes a favorite warm-weather treat for the whole family. This is best served in a glass dish or bowl to display the beautiful layers.

Serving Size: 12

Preparation & Cooking Time: 7 hours and 30 minutes

Ingredients:

- 3 cups raspberries
- 3 cups blueberries
- 2 cups strawberries, sliced
- 2 cups blackberries
- 4 teaspoons orange zest
- 1 cup orange juice
- 1 1/3 cups sugar, divided
- 1 teaspoon vanilla extract
- 16 oz. mascarpone cheese
- 1 cup heavy whipping cream
- 14 oz. ladyfinger cookies

For garnish

- Fresh berries

Instructions:

Add the raspberries, blueberries, strawberries and blackberries to a bowl.

In another bowl, mix the orange juice, orange zest and 1/3 cup sugar.

Pour this mixture over the berries and toss to coat evenly.

Cover and refrigerate for 45 minutes.

Beat the cream with an electric mixer until you see soft peaks forming.

In another bowl, add the remaining sugar.

Stir in the vanilla extract, mascarpone cheese and whipped cream.

Arrange the ladyfinger cookies in a dish.

Make several layers of the cream mixture, berry mixture and ladyfinger cookies.

Cover and refrigerate for 6 hours.

Top with the fresh berries before serving.

Nutrients per Serving:

- Calories 501
- Fat 26 g
- Saturated fat 14 g
- Carbohydrates 63 g
- Fiber 5 g
- Protein 8 g
- Cholesterol 105 mg
- Sugars 45 g
- Sodium 77 mg
- Potassium 480 mg

Colorful Gelatin Cubes

If you think these desserts are only for kids, think again. Give this a try, and you'll find yourself craving for these rainbow treats.

Serving Size: 30

Preparation & Cooking Time: 2 hours and 50 minutes

Ingredients:

- 6 packets plain gelatin, divided
- 6 packets gelatin (different flavors)
- 6 cups boiling water, divided
- 14 oz. sweetened condensed milk
- ¼ cup cold water

Instructions:

Add 1 packet each of plain and flavored gelatin to a bowl.

Do the same for the other packets in 5 other bowls, creating a total of 6 mixtures.

Add 1 cup boiling water to each bowl.

Stir until dissolved.

Pour 1 mixture into the pan and refrigerate until firm.

Do the same for the other gelatin mixture.

Stack the firm gelatin in another baking pan, alternately with a mixture of the cold water and condensed milk.

Refrigerate for 2 hours.

Slice into squares and serve.

Nutrients per Serving:

- Calories 25
- Fat 0 g
- Saturated fat 0 g
- Carbohydrates 5 g
- Fiber 0 g
- Protein 1 g
- Cholesterol 1 mg
- Sugars 5 g
- Sodium 13 mg
- Potassium 31 mg

Greek Vanilla Yogurt Cooler

This frozen treat will cool you off in an instant. And because it's very easy to make, you'll find yourself happily obliging to requests to make this treat.

Serving Size: 2

Preparation & Cooking Time: 30 minutes

Ingredients:

- 3 cups plain Greek yogurt
- ¾ cup sugar
- 1 ½ teaspoons vanilla extract
- 1 tablespoon cold water
- 1 tablespoon lemon juice
- 1 teaspoon plain gelatin

Instructions:

Line your strainer with 1 coffee filter or 4 pieces cheese cloth.

Place it over a bowl.

Add the yogurt to the strainer.

Cover and refrigerate for 2 hours.

Take the yogurt and discard the strained liquid.

Stir the sugar and vanilla.

In a heat-proof bowl, mix the lemon juice and cold water.

Add the gelatin.

Let rest for 1 minute.

Microwave it on high setting for 30 seconds.

Stir until gelatin is dissolved completely.

Let cool.

Add the gelatin mixture to the yogurt.

Cover and refrigerate for 40 minutes.

Pour the mixture into your ice cream maker.

Follow the instructions for processing.

Serve immediately or store in freezer containers.

Nutrients per Serving:

- Calories 225
- Fat 3 g
- Saturated fat 2 g
- Carbohydrates 36 g
- Fiber 0 g
- Protein 14 g
- Cholesterol 8 mg
- Sugars 36 g
- Sodium 57 mg
- Potassium 34 mg

Pineapple Cream Pie

This light and refreshing dessert is so easy that you don't have to be a kitchen expert to pull it off. You'll enjoy serving this to your friends each time they come over.

Serving Size: 8

Preparation & Cooking Time: 20 minutes

Ingredients:

- 14 oz. sweetened condensed milk
- ¼ cup lemon juice
- 8 oz. canned pineapple chunks
- 8 oz. frozen whipped topping
- 1 graham cracker crust

Toppings

- Pineapple chunks
- Macadamia nuts, toasted and chopped

Instructions:

Add the milk, lemon juice and pineapple chunks to a bowl. Mix well.

Fold in the whipped topping.

Place the crust on top of a pie pan.

Pour the mixture into the crust.

Cover and refrigerate for 10 minutes.

Top with the additional pineapple chunks and macadamia nuts before serving.

Nutrients per Serving:

- Calories 367
- Fat 14 g
- Saturated fat 9 g
- Carbohydrates 54 g
- Fiber 1 g
- Protein 5 g
- Cholesterol 17 mg
- Sugars 46 g
- Sodium 185 mg
- Potassium 292 mg

Lemon Pie

There's no need to stress over dessert! This recipe only requires 5 ingredients and only a few minutes of your time.

Serving Size: 8

Preparation & Cooking Time: 4 hours and 10 minutes

Ingredients:

- ½ cup lemon juice
- 14 oz. sweetened condensed milk
- 8 oz. cream cheese
- 1 graham cracker crust
- 2 cups whipped topping

For garnish

- Lemon slices

Instructions:

Mix the lemon juice, sweetened condensed milk and cream in a bowl.

Place the crust in a pie pan.

Pour the mixture into the crust.

Cover and refrigerate for 4 hours.

Top with the whipped topping and lemon slices before serving.

Nutrients per Serving:

- Calories 417
- Fat 22 g
- Saturated fat 13 g
- Carbohydrates 48 g
- Fiber 0 g
- Protein 7 g
- Cholesterol 46 mg
- Sugars 42 g
- Sodium 274 mg
- Potassium 285 mg

Blackberry Cheesecake Cups

Turn your favorite berry cheesecake into a dessert that you can eat right from the jar. And instead of blueberry, we use blackberry.

Serving Size: 6

Preparation & Cooking Time: 3 hours and 30 minutes

Ingredients:

- 1 ½ cups miniature pretzels
- 3 tablespoons butter, melted
- 2 tablespoons sugar
- 1 cup heavy whipping cream
- 8 oz. cream cheese
- 1 teaspoon vanilla extract
- ½ cup confectioners' sugar
- ½ cup white baking chips
- 1 ½ cups fresh blackberries, chopped
- 1/3 cup sugar

For serving

- Whipped cream
- Fresh blackberries

Instructions:

Add the pretzels to a food processor.

Process until crushed.

Stir in the butter and 2 tablespoons sugar.

Pour the mixture into a glass jar with lid.

Beat the cream with an electric mixer until you see stiff peaks forming.

In another bowl, beat the cream, vanilla extract and confectioners' sugar.

Stir in the whipped cream and baking chip.

Place the mixture on top of the pretzel mixture inside the jar.

Cover and refrigerate for 3 hours.

Add the blackberries and remaining sugar to a blender.

Process until pureed.

Add the blackberry puree to the glass jar.

Top with the additional whipped cream and blackberries.

Refrigerate for a few minutes or serve immediately

Nutrients per Serving:

- Calories 553
- Fat 38 g
- Saturated fat 23 g
- Carbohydrates 49 g
- Fiber 2 g
- Protein 6 g
- Cholesterol 102 mg
- Sugars 38 g
- Sodium 359 mg
- Potassium 309 mg

Strawberry Gelato

Each spoonful of rich, creamy, and smooth gelato will make your sweet tooth feel like it's in heaven! Give yourself this wonderful treat once in a while.

Serving Size: 12

Preparation & Cooking Time: 40 minutes

Ingredients:

- 2 cups milk
- 2 tablespoons light corn syrup
- 2 ½ cups fresh strawberries, sliced in half
- ¾ cup sugar
- 1 tablespoon honey
- ½ teaspoon salt
- ½ cup heavy whipping cream
- 1 teaspoon lemon juice

Instructions:

Add the milk, light corn syrup, strawberries, sugar, honey and salt to a blender.

Process until smooth.

Stir in the cream and process for a few more seconds.

Transfer to a bowl.

Add the lemon juice and stir.

Cover and refrigerate for 4 hours.

Transfer the mixture to your ice cream maker.

Follow the manufacturer's instructions for freezing.

Nutrients per Serving:

- Calories 160
- Fat 6 g
- Saturated fat 4 g
- Carbohydrates 26 g
- Fiber 1 g
- Protein 2 g
- Cholesterol 18 mg
- Sugars 25 g
- Sodium 124 mg
- Potassium 227 mg

Cherry & Cream Cheese Pie

You'll find this hard to believe but it only takes a few minutes and minimal effort to make this incredible pie that will surely impress everyone. Bring this to your next potluck.

Serving Size: 4

Preparation & Cooking Time: 10 minutes

Ingredients:

- 3 oz. cream cheese
- ¼ teaspoon almond extract
- ¼ cup confectioners' sugar
- 2 graham cracker shells
- ¼ cup cherry pie filling

Instructions:

Combine the cream cheese, almond extract and confectioners' sugar.

Beat until smooth.

Place the cracker shells in small plates or pans.

Top with the cream cheese mixture and cherry pie filling.

Refrigerate until ready to serve.

Nutrients per Serving:

- Calories 362
- Fat 20 g
- Saturated fat 10 g
- Carbohydrates 42 g
- Fiber 1 g
- Protein 4 g
- Cholesterol 43 mg
- Sugars 29 g
- Sodium 265 mg
- Potassium 66 mg

Banana Split Pie

Turn your favorite ice cream into a pie that's delightful to share with your family and friends. It's easy and only takes a few minutes to prepare.

Serving Size: 8

Preparation & Cooking Time: 25 minutes

Ingredients:

- 1 graham cracker crust
- 3 tablespoons chocolate-flavored hard shell topping
- 2 bananas, sliced
- ½ teaspoon lemon juice
- 1 qt. strawberry ice cream, softened
- ½ cup pineapple-flavored ice cream topping
- ½ cup chopped walnuts, toasted
- 2 cups whipped topping

For serving

- 8 maraschino cherries
- Chocolate syrup

Instructions:

Add the pie crust to a pie pan.

Pour in the chocolate topping.

Freeze for 5 minutes.

Toss the banana slices in the lemon juice.

Spread the bananas on top of the chocolate

Layer with the rest of the ingredients.

Cover and freeze for 10 to 15 minutes.

Top with the cherries and drizzle with the chocolate syrup before serving.

- Nutrients per Serving:
- Calories 459
- Fat 22 g
- Saturated fat 9 g
- Carbohydrates 64 g
- Fiber 2 g
- Protein 5 g
- Cholesterol 19 mg
- Sugars 26 g
- Sodium 174 mg
- Potassium 390 mg

Icebox Cake

This 25-minute ice box cake gives you the flavor of the tropics. Bring it to your next get-together and for sure, you'll be getting many queries about the recipe. Skip the rum if you prefer your dessert alcohol-free.

Serving Size: 12

Preparation & Cooking Time: 25 minutes

Ingredients:

- 8 oz. cream cheese
- ½ teaspoon rum extract
- ½ cup confectioners' sugar
- 14 oz. coconut milk, divided
- 3 ½ oz. instant vanilla pudding mix
- 8 oz. frozen whipped topping, thawed
- 15 graham crackers
- 20 oz. canned pineapple chunks, drained
- 1 cup coconut flakes, toasted

Instructions:

Combine the cream cheese, rum extract and confectioners' sugar in a bowl.

Beat with an electric mixer until mixture is smooth.

Stir in 1 cup coconut milk and pudding mix.

Beat until fully combined.

Fold in the thawed whipped topping.

Add the remaining coconut milk to a dish.

Dip the graham crackers in the coconut milk.

Arrange the graham crackers in a single layer in a baking pan.

Layer with the pineapple, cream cheese mixture and coconut flakes.

Repeat the layers.

Cover and refrigerate until ready to serve.

Nutrients per Serving:

- Calories 377
- Fat 20 g
- Saturated fat 15 g
- Carbohydrates 47 g
- Fiber 1 g
- Protein 3 g
- Cholesterol 19 mg
- Sugars 33 g
- Sodium 259 mg
- Potassium 236 mg

Mango Strawberry Cake

This bright and colorful cake looks like it takes a lot of work to prepare. But you'll be surprised that you can whip up something this elegant and impressive in less than an hour of active prep.

Serving Size: 12

Preparation & Cooking Time: 2 hours and 45 minutes

Ingredients:

Crust

- 2 cups graham cracker crumbs
- 1/3 cup sugar
- 2/3 cup butter, melted

Filling

- 3 tablespoons cold water
- 1 packet plain gelatin
- 16 oz. cream cheese
- 1 1/3 cups sugar
- 2 teaspoons vanilla extract
- 1 cup heavy whipping cream
- 4 fresh strawberries, chopped
- ¾ cup mango, sliced into cubes

Glaze

- 1 packet plain gelatin
- 3 tablespoons cold water
- ¾ cup mango, sliced into cubes
- ½ cup cold water

Toppings

- Whipped cream
- Mango, diced

- Strawberries, sliced

Instructions:

Prepare the crust by combining the graham cracker crumbs, sugar and melted butter in a bowl. Mix well.

Press the mixture into a cake pan.

Pour the water into a microwave-safe bowl.

Sprinkle with the gelatin.

Let sit for 1 minute.

Microwave on high setting for 10 seconds.

Stir for 1 minute.

Let cool.

In another bowl, mix the cream cheese, sugar, vanilla extract, heavy whipping cream and gelatin mixture.

Stir in the strawberries and mango.

Pour the mixture into the cake pan.

Cover and refrigerate.

Prepare the glaze by sprinkling the gelatin into 3 tablespoons cold water.

Let sit for 1 minute.

Microwave it for 10 seconds.

Stir for 1 minute.

Let cool.

Add the mango and ½ cup water to a blender or food processor.

Pulse until pureed.

Add the gelatin mixture to the mango puree.

Pour this mixture into the cake pan.

Top with the whipped cream, mango and strawberry.

Nutrients per Serving:

- Calories 495
- Fat 32 g
- Saturated fat 19 g
- Carbohydrates 48 g
- Fiber 1 g
- Protein 5 g
- Cholesterol 88 mg
- Sugars 38 g
- Sodium 285 mg
- Potassium 156 mg

Watermelon Cooler

Give yourself a refreshing treat with this watermelon cooler that only takes a few minutes of your time, and requires only 5 ingredients!

Serving Size: 4

Preparation & Cooking Time: 2 hours and 20 minutes

Ingredients:

- 2 tablespoons water
- 1 teaspoon plain gelatin
- 2 tablespoons honey
- 2 tablespoons lime juice
- 4 cups watermelon, sliced into cubes

Instructions:

Pour the water into a microwave-safe bowl.

Sprinkle the gelatin into the water.

Let sit for 1 minute.

Microwave on high setting for 30 to 40 seconds.

Stir for 2 minutes.

Add the gelatin mixture, honey, lime juice and watermelon to a blender or food processor.

Process until pureed.

Transfer to a container.

Freeze until firm.

Thaw for 15 minutes before serving.

Nutrients per Serving:

- Calories 81
- Fat 0 g
- Saturated fat 0 g
- Carbohydrates 21 g
- Fiber 1 g
- Protein 1 g
- Cholesterol 0 mg
- Sugars 18 g
- Sodium 3 mg
- Potassium 175 mg

Peanut Butter Tarts

You'll love these tarts not only for their creaminess and delicious flavors but also for the crunch you get with every spoonful.

Serving Size: 2

Preparation & Cooking Time: 1 hour and 10 minutes

Ingredients:

- 2 oz. cream cheese
- 2 tablespoons sugar
- ¼ cup peanut butter
- ¼ teaspoon vanilla extract
- 2 tablespoons sour cream
- 2 individual graham cracker shells
- 2 tablespoons whipped topping
- Peanuts, chopped

Instructions:

Combine the cream cheese, sugar and peanut butter.

Stir in the vanilla extract and sour cream.

Spoon the mixture into the graham shells.

Refrigerate for 1 to 2 hours.

Top with the whipped topping and peanuts.

Nutrients per Serving:

- Calories 500
- Fat 34 g
- Saturated fat 12 g
- Carbohydrates 39 g
- Fiber 3 g
- Protein 11 g
- Cholesterol 32 mg
- Sugars 24 g
- Sodium 375 mg
- Potassium 486 mg

Lemon Tiramisu

Can't decide between tiramisu and cheesecake? Here's a cross between those two that gives you impressive results without the exhausting work.

Serving Size: 9

Preparation & Cooking Time: 2 hours and 20 minutes

Ingredients:

- 3 ½ oz. instant lemon pudding mix
- 8 oz. cream cheese
- 8 oz. mascarpone cheese
- 1 teaspoon lemon extract
- 1 cup milk
- 2/3 cup lemon juice
- 3 tablespoons sugar
- 24 ladyfinger cookies
- 2 teaspoons lemon zest

Instructions:

Add the instant lemon pudding mix, cream cheese, mascarpone cheese, lemon extract and milk to a bowl.

Beat with an electric mixer on medium speed for 2 minutes.

Mix the lemon juice and sugar in a bowl.

Stir until the sugar has been dissolved.

Dip the ladyfinger cookies in the lemon mixture.

Arrange the ladyfinger cookies in a single layer in a baking pan.

Top with the pudding mixture.

Repeat the layers.

Sprinkle the lemon zest on top.

Cover and refrigerate for 2 hours before serving.

Nutrients per Serving:

- Calories 350
- Fat 22 g
- Saturated fat 12 g
- Carbohydrates 33 g
- Fiber 0 g
- Protein 6 g
- Cholesterol 82 mg
- Sugars 24 g
- Sodium 272 mg
- Potassium 186 mg

Watermelon & Cilantro Ice

Yes, you read it right, we combine watermelon and cilantro in this surprisingly delicious slush that you'll love.

Serving Size: 6

Preparation & Cooking Time: 4 hours and 30 minutes

Ingredients:

- ½ cup sugar
- ¼ cup water
- 4 cups watermelon, sliced into cubes
- 3 tablespoons lime juice
- 2 tablespoons pomegranate juice
- Pinch salt
- 1 tablespoon fresh cilantro, minced

Instructions:

Pour the water into a pot over medium heat.

Stir in the sugar.

Bring to a boil.

Reduce heat and simmer while stirring until the sugar has been dissolved.

Turn off heat.

Let cool.

Add the watermelon cubes to a food processor or blender.

Process until pureed.

Transfer to a bowl.

Stir in the sugar syrup, lime juice, pomegranate juice, salt and minced cilantro.

Mix well.

Refrigerate for 15 minutes.

Transfer to your ice cream maker.

Follow the manufacturer's directions for freezing.

Nutrients per Serving:

- Calories 93
- Fat 0.1 g
- Saturated Fat 0.1 g
- Carbohydrate 24.3 g
- Fiber 0.4 g
- Cholesterol 0 mg
- Protein 0.6 g
- Sugars 22.9 g
- Sodium 29 mg
- Potassium 114 mg

Berry Cheesecake Parfait

This berry cheesecake parfait is not only eye candy but also a refreshingly good dessert that's very easy to prepare. You'll love the sweet-sour flavors, the creamy layers and the crunchiness of the crushed graham crackers.

Serving Size: 2

Preparation & Cooking Time: 15 minutes

Ingredients:

- 2/3 cup marshmallow cream
- 2 oz. cream cheese, softened
- ½ cup frozen whipped topping
- 4 tablespoons crushed graham cracker
- 1 cup blueberries
- 1 cup raspberries

Instructions:

Combine the marshmallow cream and cream cheese in a bowl.

Beat until smooth.

Fold in the frozen whipped topping.

Layer the glass jars with the crushed graham crackers, cream cheese mixture and berries.

Refrigerate until ready to serve.

Nutrients per Serving:

- Calories 396
- Fat 15 g
- Saturated fat 9 g
- Carbohydrates 54 g
- Fiber 6 g
- Protein 4 g
- Cholesterol 29 mg
- Sugars 39 g
- Sodium 174 mg
- Potassium 319 mg

Strawberry & Lemon Pie

The divine goodness of this strawberry lemonade pie will leave you speechless! This is the recipe to show you that lemon and strawberry are a good combination for a no-bake summer dessert.

Serving Size: 8

Preparation & Cooking Time: 2 hours and 15 minutes

Ingredients:

- 2 ½ cups frozen strawberries, sliced
- 3 ½ oz. instant lemon pudding mix
- 8 oz. frozen whipped topping, thawed
- 1 graham cracker crust

Topping

- Whipped topping
- Strawberries, sliced

Instructions:

Mix the strawberries and instant pudding mix in a bowl.

Let sit for 5 minutes.

Stir in the whipped topping.

Spoon and spread the mixture into the graham crust.

Freeze for 4 hours.

Top with whipped topping and strawberries before serving.

Nutrients per Serving:

- Calories 306

- Fat 10 g

- Saturated fat 6 g

- Carbohydrates 51 g

- Fiber 2 g

- Protein 1 g

- Cholesterol 0 mg

- Sugars 45 g

- Sodium 273 mg

- Potassium 88 mg

Almond Butter Ice Cream

This dairy-free ice cream is a special treat for everyone. It's a great way to cool off during hot summer days.

Serving Size: 8

Preparation & Cooking Time: 4 hours and 10 minutes

Ingredients:

- 1 cup almond milk (unsweetened)
- 2 cups coconut milk
- ½ cup almond butter
- ½ cup sugar
- ½ teaspoon sea salt
- ½ cup chocolate chips, melted

Instructions:

Add the almond milk, coconut milk, almond butter, sugar and salt to a bowl.

Mix well.

Transfer the mixture to your ice cream maker.

Follow the manufacturer's instructions for freezing.

Add the melted chocolate in the last 3 minutes.

Freeze for 4 hours.

Nutrients per Serving:

- Calories 316
- Fat 25.1 g
- Saturated Fat 21.2 g
- Carbohydrate 23.9 g
- Fiber 2.4 g
- Protein 3.1 g
- Cholesterol 2 mg
- Sugars 21 g
- Sodium 139 mg
- Potassium 283 mg

Lime Cheesecake

This is another kind of no-bake dessert that's a cinch to prepare but at the same time guarantees compliments from anyone who gives it a try.

Serving Size: 12

Preparation & Cooking Time: 4 hours and 30 minutes

Ingredients:

- 32 ladyfinger cookies, split
- ¼ cup lime juice
- 1 packet plain gelatin
- 1 cup sugar
- 16 oz. cream cheese
- 6 oz. white baking chocolate, melted
- 2 teaspoons lime zest
- 1 cup heavy whipping cream, whipped

Topping

- Fresh lime slices
- Fresh strawberry slices

Instructions:

Arrange the ladyfinger cookies on the bottom and edges of your cake pan.

Pour the lime juice into a bowl.

Sprinkle the gelatin on top.

Let sit for 1 minute.

Transfer the mixture to a pan over low heat.

Stir until the gelatin has been dissolved. Let it cool.

Beat the sugar and cream cheese in a bowl.

Stir in the gelatin mixture, melted white chocolate and lime zest.

Fold in the whipped cream.

Pour the mixture into the cake pan.

Refrigerate for 3 to 4 hours.

Garnish with the fresh lime and strawberry slices before serving.

Nutrients per Serving:

- Calories 408
- Fat 25 g
- Saturated fat 16 g
- Carbohydrates 42 g
- Fiber 0 g
- Protein 6 g
- Cholesterol 100 mg
- Sugars 35 g
- Sodium 103 mg
- Potassium 88 mg

Peanut Butter Cream Pie

This fantastic no-bake dessert features creamy peanut butter filling, crunchy crust and crunchy topping that certainly won't leave you wanting.

Serving Size: 8

Preparation & Cooking Time: 4 hours and 10 minutes

Ingredients:

- 8 oz. cream cheese
- ½ cup peanut butter
- ¾ cup confectioners' sugar
- 8 oz. frozen whipped topping
- 6 tablespoons milk
- 1 graham cracker crust
- ¼ cup peanuts, chopped

Instructions:

Combine the cream cheese until fluffy.

Stir in the peanut butter and sugar.

Fold in the whipped topping and milk.

Place the crust in a pie pan.

Spread the mixture on top of the crust.

Top with the chopped peanuts.

Cover and refrigerate for 4 hours before serving.

Nutrients per Serving:

- Calories 456
- Fat 31 g
- Saturated fat 14 g
- Carbohydrates 37 g
- Fiber 2 g
- Protein 9 g
- Cholesterol 33 mg
- Sugars 26 g
- Sodium 304 mg
- Potassium 245 mg

Raspberry Cream Pie

This raspberry cream pie easily becomes a favorite comfort food! You'll relish the fresh raspberries, luscious creamy filling and buttery crust.

Serving Size: 8

Preparation & Cooking Time: 30 minutes

Ingredients:

- 1 ½ cups vanilla wafers, crushed
- 1/3 cup pecans, chopped
- ¼ cup butter, melted

Filling

- 8 oz. cream cheese
- 2 tablespoons orange liqueur
- 1 teaspoon vanilla extract
- 2/3 cup confectioners' sugar
- 1 cup heavy whipping cream

Topping

- 1 ½ cups raspberries, divided
- 3 tablespoons cornstarch
- 1 cup sugar
- 3 tablespoons water

Garnish

- ½ cup raspberries

Instructions:

Mix the pecans, crushed wafers and butter in a bowl.

Press the mixture into a pie plate.

In a bowl, beat the cream cheese, orange liqueur, vanilla extract and confectioners' sugar.

Stir in the heavy whipping cream.

Spread the mixture on top of the crust.

Refrigerate for 30 minutes.

Add the raspberries to a blender.

Process until pureed.

Transfer to a saucepan over medium low heat.

Stir in the cornstarch, sugar and water.

Simmer for 2 to 3 minutes.

Turn off heat and let cool.

Refrigerate for 30 minutes.

Spread the mixture on top of the pie.

Garnish with the whole raspberries.

Nutrients per Serving:

- Calories 507
- Fat 28 g
- Saturated fat 14 g
- Carbohydrates 61 g
- Fiber 4 g
- Protein 4 g
- Cholesterol 70 mg
- Sugars 46 g
- Sodium 196 mg
- Potassium 97 mg

Lemon Cheesecake Tart

These mini tarts are semi-homemade no-bake desserts quickly made with prepared pie crust, topped with lemon curd and fresh blueberries.

Serving Size: 12

Preparation & Cooking Time: 2 hours and 10 minutes

Ingredients:

- 2 sheets prepared pie crust

Filling

- 8 oz. cream cheese
- 10 oz. lemon curd
- 1 teaspoon vanilla extract
- 8 oz. frozen whipped topping
- 1 cup fresh blueberries

Topping

- Confectioners' sugar

Instructions:

Cut round shapes from the pie crust using a cookie cutter.

Press each one into a muffin cup.

Mix the filling ingredients, except blueberries.

Pour the mixture into the shell.

Top with the blueberries.

Refrigerate for 2 hours.

Sprinkle with the confectioners' sugar before serving.

Nutrients per Serving:

- Calories 166
- Fat 9 g
- Saturated fat 5 g
- Carbohydrates 18 g
- Fiber 0 g
- Protein 1 g
- Cholesterol 22 mg
- Sugars 10 g
- Sodium 95 mg
- Potassium 86 mg

Chocolate Caramel Pie with Hazelnuts

This pie is loaded with a sweet tooth's favorites—caramel, chocolate, creamy filling and crispy crust. You'll also fall in love with how perfectly the hazelnuts go with the rest of the ingredients of this heavenly pie.

Serving Size: 8

Preparation & Cooking Time: 4 hours and 30 minutes

Ingredients:

- 12 shortbread cookies
- 1 ½ cups caramel pretzels
- ¼ cup sugar
- 6 tablespoons butter, melted
- 5 tablespoons caramel syrup, divided

Filling

- ½ cup hazelnut cocoa spread
- 8 oz. cream cheese
- 8 oz. frozen whipped topping
- 7 oz. marshmallow cream
- 1 chocolate bar, chopped
- 1 cup mini marshmallows

Instructions:

Add the shortbread cookies and caramel pretzels to your food processor.

Pulse until crumbly.

Stir in the melted butter and sugar.

Press the crust into a pie pan.

Drizzle with 3 tablespoons caramel syrup.

Freeze for 15 minutes.

Prepare the filling by mixing the cream cheese, hazelnut cocoa spread, whipped topping, and marshmallow cream.

Fold in the chocolate pieces and marshmallows.

Spread the mixture on top of the crust.

Refrigerate for 4 hours.

Top with the remaining caramel syrup before serving.

Nutrients per Serving:

- Calories 663
- Fat 35 g
- Saturated fat 19 g
- Carbohydrates 74 g
- Fiber 1 g
- Protein 6 g
- Cholesterol 60 mg
- Sugars 57 g
- Sodium 327 mg
- Potassium 316 mg

Frozen Peach Pie

The rich and creamy peach filling and the buttery graham crust will definitely make you go wow. This peach pie is surprisingly easy to make.

Serving Size: 16

Preparation & Cooking Time: 4 hours and 30 minutes

Ingredients:

- 2 ½ cups graham cracker, crushed
- ¼ cup sugar
- ½ cup butter, melted
- 14 oz. condensed milk
- ¼ cup orange juice
- ¼ cup lemon juice
- 1 tablespoon lemon zest
- 16 oz. peaches, sliced
- 1 ½ cups heavy whipping cream
- Whipped cream

Instructions:

Mix the crushed graham crackers, sugar and butter in a bowl.

Press the mixture into a pie pan.

Freeze for 15 minutes.

Add the condensed milk, orange juice, lemon juice, lemon zest and peaches to a blender or food processor.

Process until smooth.

Transfer to a bowl.

In another bowl, beat the cream with an electric mixer until you see stiff peaks forming.

Fold this into the peach mixture.

Spread the mixture onto the crust.

Cover and freeze for 4 hours.

Top with the whipped cream before serving.

Nutrients per Serving:

- Calories 302
- Fat 19 g
- Saturated fat 11 g
- Carbohydrates 31 g
- Fiber 1 g
- Protein 4 g
- Cholesterol 58 mg
- Sugars 23 g
- Sodium 170 mg
- Potassium 417 mg

Cheesecake Berry Parfait

A delightful change to the usual fruit parfait that you serve during get-together—this is one no-bake dessert that won't tire you out but will definitely give your guests a good reason to thank you endlessly for dinner.

Serving Size: 2

Preparation & Cooking Time: 15 minutes

Ingredients:

- 2 oz cream cheese, softened
- 4 teaspoons sugar
- 2/3 cup whipped topping
- ½ cup blueberries
- ½ cup raspberries
- ½ cup strawberries
- Whipped topping

Instructions:

Beat the cream cheese in a bowl.

Stir in the sugar and whipped topping.

Layer ¼ of the mixture in a glass.

Top with the berries.

Repeat layers.

Top with the whipped topping.

Refrigerate until ready to serve.

Nutrients per Serving:

- Calories 146
- Fat 4 g
- Saturated fat 4 g
- Carbohydrates 25 g
- Fiber 3 g
- Protein 1 g
- Cholesterol 0 mg
- Sugars 21 g
- Sodium 1 mg
- Potassium 173 mg

Blueberry Cheesecake

Yes, you can make this popular dessert without going near any oven. This no-bake dessert comes in handy when you're running behind your schedule.

Serving Size: 4

Preparation & Cooking Time: 4 hours and 30 minutes

Ingredients:2

- tablespoons butter, melted
- ¾ cup vanilla wafers, crushed

Filling

- 2 tablespoons cold water
- 1 ¼ teaspoons plain gelatin
- 8 oz. cream cheese
- 1 ½ teaspoons lemon juice
- ½ teaspoon lemon zest
- 1 ½ cups whipped topping
- 1 cup marshmallow cream
- 1 cup blueberries

Instructions:

Mix the butter and crushed wafers.

Press this onto a pie pan.

Pour the cold water into a pan.

Sprinkle the gelatin over the water.

Let sit for 1 minute.

Put the pan over low heat.

Heat through while stirring until the gelatin has been dissolved.

Turn off heat and let cool.

Add the cream cheese to a bowl.

Stir in the gelatin mixture.

Add the rest lemon juice, lemon zest, whipped topping and marshmallow cream.

Mix well.

Add the blueberries to a blender or food processor.

Process until pureed.

Add this to the cream cheese mixture.

Spread the mixture on top of the crust.

Cover and refrigerate for at least 4 hours.

Nutrients per Serving:

- Calories 523
- Fat 34 g
- Saturated fat 21 g
- Carbohydrates 49 g
- Fiber 1 g
- Protein 6 g
- Cholesterol 79 mg
- Sugars 32 g
- Sodium 318 mg
- Potassium 248 mg

Peanut Butter Cup Trifle

For a sweet and delicious afternoon, prepare this delicious peanut butter cup trifle. It's just the right amount of sweet and creamy that you'd love.

Serving Size: 12

Preparation & Cooking Time: 1 hour and 10 minutes

Ingredients:

- 8 oz. instant chocolate pudding mix
- 4 cups cold milk
- 10 oz. angel food cake, prepared and sliced into cubes
- 12 oz. frozen whipped topping, thawed
- 16 oz. mini peanut butter cups

Instructions:

Combine the pudding mix and cold milk in a bowl.

Stir for 2 minutes.

Let sit for another 2 minutes.

Layer a trifle bowl with angel food cake pieces, pudding, whipped topping and mini peanut butter cups.

Repeat the layers.

Refrigerate for at least 1 hour or until ready to serve.

Nutrients per Serving:

- Calories 174
- Fat 8.2 g
- Saturated Fat 5 g
- Carbohydrate 21.2 g
- Fiber 0.4 g
- Cholesterol 28 mg
- Protein 5 g
- Sugars 5.9 g
- Sodium 252 mg
- Potassium 110 mg

Macaroon Ice Cream Torte

This frozen treat is so good your friends will surely be impressed. Layers of chocolate topped with crunchy toffee bits and drizzled with hot fudge syrup—this is truly a slice of heaven.

Serving Size: 16

Preparation & Cooking Time: 4 hours and 20 minutes

Ingredients:

- 30 macaroon cookies, crushed
- 1 qt. chocolate ice cream
- 1 qt. coffee ice cream
- 1 cup chocolate toffee, chopped
- Hot fudge syrup

Instructions:

Layer 1/3 of the crushed cookies in a cake pan.

Layer with the coffee and chocolate ice cream.

Add another layer of the cookies.

Repeat the layers.

Sprinkle with the toffee bits on top.

Cover and freeze for 4 hours.

Drizzle with the hot fudge syrup before serving.

Nutrients per Serving:

- Calories 341
- Fat 20 g
- Saturated fat 11 g
- Carbohydrates 37 g
- Fiber 2 g
- Protein 4 g
- Cholesterol 36 mg
- Sugars 35 g
- Sodium 110 mg
- Potassium 129 mg

Rocky Road Pie

Rocky road can also refer to a pie aside from being a popular option for ice cream flavor. This pie is typically made with chocolate and marshmallows. You can also make it with pecans, almonds, or walnuts.

Serving Size: 8

Preparation & Cooking Time: 6 hours and 15 minutes

Ingredients:

- 1 ½ cups half and half cream
- 4 oz. instant chocolate pudding mix
- 8 oz. frozen whipped topping, thawed
- ¼ cup mini marshmallows
- ½ cup pecans, chopped
- 1/3 cup chocolate chips
- 1 graham cracker crust

Topping

- Chopped pecans
- Mini marshmallows
- Chocolate syrup

Instructions:

Combine the cream and chocolate pudding mix in a bowl.

Stir for 2 minutes.

Fold in the thawed whipped topping.

Fold in the marshmallows, pecans and chocolate chips.

Add the graham crust to a pie pan.

Spread the mixture on top of the crust.

Freeze for 6 hours.

Take it out of the freezer at least 10 to 15 minutes before serving.

Nutrients per Serving:

- Calories 184
- Fat 10 g
- Saturated fat 5 g
- Carbohydrates 20 g
- Fiber 1 g
- Protein 2 g
- Cholesterol 11 mg
- Sugars 15 g
- Sodium 175 mg
- Potassium 153 mg

Berry Cheesecake

If you're looking for a cheesecake recipe that won't eat up much of your time, here's the recipe for you. It's also very easy that you don't have to be a kitchen pro to get this done the right way.

Serving Size: 12

Preparation & Cooking Time: 1 day, 4 hours and 50 minutes

Ingredients:

- 1 ½ cups graham crackers, crushed
- ½ teaspoon ground cinnamon
- ½ cup butter, melted
- 1/3 cup brown sugar

Filling

- 16 oz. cream cheese
- 2 teaspoons lemon juice
- 1/3 cup sugar
- 2 cups heavy whipping cream

Topping

- 1 cup raspberries
- 1 cup blueberries
- 2 cups strawberries, sliced
- 2 tablespoons sugar

Instructions:

Combine the crushed graham, ground cinnamon, melted butter and brown sugar.

Press the crust onto a pie pan.

Cover and refrigerate for 30 to 40 minutes.

Beat the cream cheese, lemon juice and sugar in a bowl.

Stir in the cream.

Beat until you see stiff peaks forming.

Spread this on top of the crust.

Cover and refrigerate overnight.

Sprinkle the berries with the sugar.

Let sit for 30 minutes.

Top the cheesecake with the berries and serve.

Nutrients per Serving:

- Calories 432
- Fat 34 g
- Saturated fat 21 g
- Carbohydrates 29 g
- Fiber 2 g
- Protein 5 g
- Cholesterol 109 mg
- Sugars 20 g
- Sodium 229 mg
- Potassium 165 mg

Peanut Butter Chocolate Pie

Peanut butter and chocolate are undeniably one of the best pairing desserts I have ever seen. And you'll love making this no-bake dessert recipe because it gives you stellar results without consuming much of your time.

Serving Size: 16

Preparation & Cooking Time: 4 hours and 30 minutes

Ingredients:

- 20 chocolate sandwich cookies, divided
- 8 oz. cream cheese
- 1 ½ cups confectioners' sugar, divided
- 2 tablespoons butter
- 4 oz. instant chocolate fudge pudding mix
- 15 mini peanut butter cups, chopped
- ½ cup peanut butter
- 16 oz. frozen whipped topping, thawed and divided
- 1 cup milk

Instructions:

Crush 15 chocolate sandwich cookies.

Toss the crushed cookies in butter.

Press the mixture into a baking pan. Set aside.

Beat the cream cheese and peanut butter in a bowl.

Stir in 1 cup confectioners' sugar.

Fold in 8 ounces whipped topping.

Spread the mixture on top of the crust.

Top with the peanut butter cups.

In another bowl, beat the milk, remaining confectioners' sugar and pudding mix using an electric mixer.

Beat for 2 minutes on low speed.

Let sit for another 2 minutes.

Fold in the remaining whipped topping.

Spread the mixture on top of the peanut butter cups.

Crush the remaining chocolate sandwich cookies.

Sprinkle these on top.

Cover and refrigerate for 4 hours.

Nutrients per Serving:

- Calories 365
- Fat 20 g
- Saturated fat 11 g
- Carbohydrates 39 g
- Fiber 1 g
- Protein 5 g
- Cholesterol 20 mg
- Sugars 33 g
- Sodium 130 mg
- Potassium 155 mg

Pretzel Dessert

Any dessert lover will say yes to this fantastic sweet treat that's not just delicious but also filling and easy to make.

Serving Size: 16

Preparation & Cooking Time: 30 minutes

Ingredients:

- 2 cups pretzels, crushed and divided
- ¾ cup butter, melted
- ¾ cup sugar
- 8 oz. cream cheese
- 1 cup confectioners' sugar
- 8 oz. frozen whipped topping, thawed
- 21 oz. cherry pie filling

Instructions:

Toss 1 ½ cups pretzels in the butter and sugar.

Press the mixture onto a baking pan.

In a bowl, mix the cream cheese, confectioners' sugar and whipped topping.

Add half of this mixture on top of the pretzel crust.

Layer with the pie filling.

Add another layer of the cream cheese mixture.

Top with the remaining pretzels.

Cover and refrigerate until ready to serve.

Nutrients per Serving:

- Calories 314
- Fat 16 g
- Saturated fat 11 g
- Carbohydrates 40 g
- Fiber 1 g
- Protein 2 g
- Cholesterol 38 mg
- Sugars 19 g
- Sodium 290 mg
- Potassium 99 mg

Blueberry Angel No-Bake Cake

It doesn't get any easier than this blueberry angel cake that doesn't require too much time and effort. You'll have impressive dessert on the table in no time.

Serving Size: 12

Preparation & Cooking Time: 2 hours and 10 minutes

Ingredients:

- 8 oz. cream cheese
- 1 cup confectioners' sugar
- 10 oz. angel food cake, prepared and sliced into cubes
- 8 oz. frozen whipped topping, thawed
- 21 oz. blueberry pie filling

Instructions:

Add the cream cheese and confectioners' sugar to a bowl.

Mix until smooth.

Gently stir in the cake pieces and whipped topping.

Spread the mixture into a baking pan.

Top with the blueberry pie filling.

Cover and refrigerate for 2 hours.

Nutrients per Serving:

- Calories 382
- Fat 10 g
- Saturated fat 7 g
- Carbohydrates 70 g
- Fiber 3 g
- Protein 3 g
- Cholesterol 21 mg
- Sugars 50 g
- Sodium 223 mg
- Potassium 162 mg

Mini S'mores

S'mores are campfire treats that well-loved in Canada and the United States. To make these, you'll have to stack together graham crackers, chocolate, and marshmallows. In this recipe, we make it without the campfire, and we give a little twist to this classic treat.

Serving Size: 12

Preparation & Cooking Time: 40 minutes

Ingredients:

- ¼ cup cold butter, sliced into cubes
- 10 oz. mini marshmallows
- 1 ½ cups graham crackers, crushed
- 6 cups rice crispies
- 1 cup chocolate chips

Frosting

- ¾ cup butter, softened
- 1 cup confectioners' sugar
- 7 oz. marshmallow cream

Topping

- ¼ cup graham crackers, crushed
- Chocolate candy bars, divided

Instructions:

Add the butter to a pot over medium heat.

Stir in the marshmallows.

Cook while stirring until marshmallows have melted.

Turn off heat.

Stir in the crushed graham and rice crispies.

Fold in the chocolate chips.

Spread the mixture in a baking pan.

Let cool.

Prepare the frosting by beating the butter and confectioners' sugar.

Stir in the marshmallow cream.

Beat with an electric mixer on low speed.

Spread the frosting on top of the bars.

Slice the bars.

Top with the chocolate.

Nutrients per Serving:

- Calories 270
- Fat 12 g
- Saturated fat 7 g
- Carbohydrates 40 g
- Fiber 1 g
- Protein 2 g
- Cholesterol 23 mg
- Sugars 26 g
- Sodium 158 mg
- Potassium 88 mg

Butterfinger Bites

Create these decadent treats that won't keep you inside the kitchen for long hours. Be sure to make a big batch, as everyone's going to love these butterfinger bites.

Serving Size: 24

Preparation & Cooking Time: 50 minutes

Ingredients:

- 1 cup candy corn
- 2/3 cup peanut butter
- 1 teaspoon coconut oil
- 1 cup chocolate syrup

Instructions:

Add the candy corn to a microwave safe bowl.

Microwave on high setting for 30 seconds.

Stir in the peanut butter.

Microwave on high setting 1 minute.

Stir until smooth.

Shape the mixture into balls.

Place on a baking sheet lined with waxed paper.

Mix the coconut oil and chocolate syrup in another bowl.

Dip the balls in the mixture.

Refrigerate until ready to serve.

Nutrients per Serving:

- Calories 50
- Fat 3 g
- Saturated fat 1 g
- Carbohydrates 6 g
- Fiber 0 g
- Protein 1 g
- Cholesterol 0 mg
- Sugars 6 g
- Sodium 16 mg
- Potassium 75 mg

Strawberry Sorbet

This is another sensational dessert that you can come up with. This requires long hours of freezing but the actual preparation is only for a few minutes.

Serving Size: 8

Preparation & Cooking Time: 4 hours and 20 minutes

Ingredients:

- 2 cups strawberry sorbet, softened
- 1 oz. instant vanilla pudding mix
- 1 cup nonfat milk
- 8 oz. low-fat whipped topping
- 1 cup strawberry, sliced

Instructions:

Line your loaf pan with foil or plastic wrap.

Spread the sorbet in the bottom of the pan.

Freeze for 15 minutes.

Combine the pudding mix and milk in a bowl.

Let sit for 2 minutes.

Stir in the whipped topping.

Spread this mixture on top of the sorbet.

Freeze for 4 hours.

Take it out of the freezer 10 minutes before serving.

Invert onto a serving platter.

Slice and top with the strawberry.

Nutrients per Serving:

- Calories 153
- Fat 3 g
- Saturated fat 3 g
- Carbohydrates 27 g
- Fiber 2 g
- Protein 1 g
- Cholesterol 1 mg
- Sugars 18 g
- Sodium 163 mg
- Potassium 142 mg

Cherry & Coconut Bars

Layer after layer of decadence—these cherry and coconut bars are guaranteed to please any sweet tooth.

Serving Size: 16

Preparation & Cooking Time: 2 hours

Ingredients:

- 1 ½ cups mini marshmallows
- 3 cups graham crackers, crushed
- ½ cup maraschino cherries, chopped
- 1 cup coconut flakes
- 1 teaspoon maple flavoring
- 14 oz. condensed milk

Frosting

- 1 cup brown sugar
- 1/3 cup butter, sliced into cubes
- ¼ cup milk
- 1 cup confectioners' sugar

Instructions:

Combine the mini marshmallows, graham crackers, maraschino cherries, coconut flakes, maple flavoring and condensed milk in a bowl.

Stir well.

Spread the mixture onto a baking pan.

Add the frosting ingredients except confectioners' sugar to a pan over medium heat.

Bring to a boil.

Reduce heat and keep stirring for 3 minutes.

Transfer to a bowl.

Let cool for 15 minutes.

Stir in the confectioners' sugar.

Spread this mixture on top of the graham crust.

Refrigerate for 1 hour and 30 minutes.

Slice into bars and serve.

Nutrients per Serving:

- Calories 169
- Fat 6 g
- Saturated fat 4 g
- Carbohydrates 28 g
- Fiber 1 g
- Protein 2 g
- Cholesterol 9 mg
- Sugars 22 g
- Sodium 82 mg
- Potassium 128 mg

Chocolate & Pretzel Bars

It has been proven countless times that chocolate and pretzels go well together. Here's another proof of this delicious combination.

Serving Size: 12

Preparation & Cooking Time: 50 minutes

Ingredients:

- 3 cups mini pretzels, broken and divided
- 10 oz. mini marshmallows
- 3 cups rice cereal
- 6 tablespoons butter, melted
- ½ cup light corn syrup, divided
- 2 tablespoons butter
- ¾ cup peanut butter chips, melted
- 1 cup chocolate chips, melted
- ¼ cup peanuts, roasted and chopped

Instructions:

Add 2 ½ cups pretzels, marshmallows and rice cereals to a bowl.

Drizzle with the melted butter.

Spread the mixture onto a baking pan.

Add half of the corn syrup and butter to a microwave-safe bowl.

Microwave on high for 60 seconds.

Stir in the peanut butter chips.

Microwave for another 30 seconds.

Spread this mixture on top of the cereal mixture.

Mix the remaining corn syrup, melted chocolate and melted peanut butter.

Spread this on the top most layer.

Press the remaining pretzels and peanuts on top.

Cover and chill in the refrigerator for 30 minutes.

Slice and serve.

Nutrients per Serving:

- Calories 136
- Fat 6 g
- Saturated fat 3 g
- Carbohydrates 20 g
- Fiber 1 g
- Protein 2 g
- Cholesterol 8 mg
- Sugars 10 g
- Sodium 124 mg
- Potassium 77 mg

Trail Mix Dessert

Here's a dessert version of your favorite trail mix. It's fun, colorful and simple to prepare.

Serving Size: 12

Preparation & Cooking Time: 30 minutes

Ingredients:

- 1 cup corn cereal
- 2 cups chocolate candies
- 2 ½ cups pretzel sticks, broken in half
- 1/3 cup peanut butter
- ½ cup butter
- 5 cups min marshmallows

Instructions:

Toss the cereal, chocolate candies and pretzels in a bowl.

Add the peanut butter and butter to a pan over medium heat.

Stir until melted.

Stir in the marshmallows.

Cook while stirring until smooth.

Pour the mixture into the bowl.

Spread the mixture into a baking pan.

Let cool until firm.

Slice and serve.

Nutrients per Serving:

- Calories 114
- Fat 6 g
- Saturated fat 3 g
- Carbohydrates 15 g
- Fiber 0 g
- Protein 2 g
- Cholesterol 8 mg
- Sugars 9 g
- Sodium 107 mg
- Potassium 49 mg

Lemon & Blueberry Trifle

This majestic dessert would make anyone ask what the special occasion is but it's actually a cinch to prepare. It also requires only a handful of ingredients.

Serving Size: 14

Preparation & Cooking Time: 2 hours and 10 minutes

Ingredients:

- 2 cups lemon yogurt
- 15 ¾ oz. lemon pie filling
- 1 angel food cake, prepared, sliced into cubes and divided
- 3 cups blueberries, divided
- 8 oz. frozen whipped topping, thawed

Instructions:

Add the lemon yogurt and lemon pie filling to a bowl.

Layer 1/3 of the angel food cake cubes in the trifle bowl.

Add layers of the yogurt mixture, blueberries and whipped topping.

Repeat the layers.

Cover and refrigerate for 2 hours.

Nutrients per Serving:

- Calories 230
- Fat 4 g
- Saturated fat 3 g
- Carbohydrates 44 g
- Fiber 1 g
- Protein 3 g
- Cholesterol 2 mg
- Sugars 27 g
- Sodium 235 mg
- Potassium 235 mg

Orange & Strawberry Pops

You can't go wrong with these orange and strawberry pops that will cool you off on the hottest summer days.

Serving Size: 10

Preparation & Cooking Time: 6 hours and 20 minutes

Ingredients:

- 6 tablespoons water
- 2 cups strawberries, sliced
- 1 tablespoon sugar
- 2 cups oranges, sliced and seeded
- 6 tablespoons orange juice

Instructions:

Pour the water into a blender.

Add the strawberries and sugar.

Process until pureed.

Add the mixture to popsicle molds.

Freeze for 2 hours.

Add the oranges and orange juice.

Freeze for 4 hours.

Nutrients per Serving:

- Calories 82
- Fat 0 g
- Saturated fat 0 g
- Carbohydrates 20 g
- Fiber 3 g
- Protein 1 g
- Cholesterol 0 mg
- Sugars 16 g
- Sodium 3 mg
- Potassium 178 mg

Raspberry Ice Cream Cake

This is a delightful way to cap your meal. This raspberry ice cream cake is not only cool and refreshing but also sweet and decadent.

Serving Size: 15

Preparation & Cooking Time: 4 hours and 30 minutes

Ingredients:

- 2 cups chocolate wafers, crushed
- 1/3 cup butter, melted
- ¼ cup sugar

Filling

- 1 cup hot fudge syrup
- 1 qt. vanilla ice cream
- 1 qt. raspberry sorbet
- 10 oz. frozen raspberries, thawed
- 8 oz. frozen whipped topping, thawed

Instructions:

Combine the crushed wafers, butter and sugar.

Reserve ¼ cup of this mixture.

Press the mixture into a baking pan.

Freeze for 15 minutes.

Spread the hot fudge syrup on top of the crust.

Spread the ice cream on top.

Add the sorbet on top of the ice cream.

Sprinkle with the raspberries and reserved wafer mixture on top.

Top with the whipped topping.

Cover and freeze for 2 hours.

Take out of the freezer 10 minutes before serving.

Nutrients per Serving:

- Calories 342
- Fat 14 g
- Saturated fat 9 g
- Carbohydrates 50 g
- Fiber 2 g
- Protein 4 g
- Cholesterol 28 mg
- Sugars 27 g
- Sodium 192 mg
- Potassium 135 mg

Conclusion

Do not let the hot summer months stop you from enjoying your favorite food.

Take advantage of the fresh ingredients that are abundant in the summertime to load up on essential nutrients.

No-bake options make cooking quick, simple, and more enjoyable.

Take it easy this summer and savor the luscious oven-free recipes this cookbook has in store.

About the Author

A native of Albuquerque, New Mexico, Sophia Freeman found her calling in the culinary arts when she enrolled at the Sante Fe School of Cooking. Freeman decided to take a year after graduation and travel around Europe, sampling the cuisine from small bistros and family owned restaurants from Italy to Portugal. Her bubbly personality and inquisitive nature made her popular with the locals in the villages and when she finished her trip and came home, she had made friends for life in the places she had visited. She also came home with a deeper understanding of European cuisine.

Freeman went to work at one of Albuquerque's 5-star restaurants as a sous-chef and soon worked her way up to head chef. The restaurant began to feature Freeman's original dishes as specials on the menu and soon after, she began to write e-books with her recipes. Sophia's dishes mix local flavours with European inspiration making them irresistible to the diners in her restaurant and the online community.

Freeman's experience in Europe didn't just teach her new ways of cooking, but also unique methods of presentation. Using rich sauces, crisp vegetables and meat cooked to perfection, she creates a stunning display as well as a delectable dish. She has won many local awards for her cuisine and she continues to delight her diners with her culinary masterpieces.

Author's Afterthoughts

I want to convey my big thanks to all of my readers who have taken the time to read my book. Readers like you make my work so rewarding and I cherish each and every one of you.

Grateful cannot describe how I feel when I know that someone has chosen my work over all of the choices available online. I hope you enjoyed the book as much as I enjoyed writing it.

Feedback from my readers is how I grow and learn as a chef and an author. Please take the time to let me know your thoughts by leaving a review on Amazon so I and your fellow readers can learn from your experience.

My deepest thanks,

Sophia Freeman

https://sophia.subscribemenow.com/